The "Voice" of Worship

The "Voice" of Worship

A Guide for the Contemporary Worship Singer

KELLY F. MCDOWELL

WIPF & STOCK · Eugene, Oregon

Wipf & Stock
An Imprint of Wipf and Stock Publishers
199 W. 8th Ave., Suite 3
Eugene, OR 97401

www.wipfandstock.com

PAPERBACK ISBN: 979-8-3852-0682-7
HARDCOVER ISBN: 979-8-3852-0683-4
EBOOK ISBN: 979-8-3852-0684-1

02/08/24

Contents

Preface

IT IS SUNDAY MORNING, and you're up before the rest of the family. You are working hard to stay quiet as you get showered and ready to head out the door. It's a bit of a chore to get presentable, quietly all while preparing your heart and soul for a worship mindset. The church parking lot is dark as you arrive hours before service begins, and your only companions in the parking lot are the sleepy eyes of your fellow bandmates, production servers, and coffee attendants. Rehearsal has the normal bumps for an early morning practice as people iron out the sleep in their steps, fingers, and voices.

Service is about to start. The team walks out prepared to lead the people into the presence of God. Through the music you fight between fully worshiping and being slightly distracted by the issues your voice just can't seem to work out. That one bridge is just a little high and your voice threatens a crack. Maybe your choir-trained voice struggles to sound like the contemporary artist you want to be, or you just can't seem to get on top of the pitch. The congregation never seems to notice, but you wish there was more you could do. After service, you reflect on the morning. It went well enough, and people appeared to be connecting authentically with the Savior (which is the goal), but you wish it could be just a bit easier, more natural, and flowy.

It can. Singing does not have to be a chore. It is a tool the Creator has given his people to use to express the feelings and emotions that seem to escape words. With a bit of instruction and some personal work time, your vocal worship leading can become more worship and less work. This book is designed to help you gain some of the technical skills you may benefit from to help the task become more natural and emotive. With a bit of training, you can refine your technique so you can release your body and mind to focus on what you have been called to do, lead others into the presence and in the worship of the Lord most high.

Acknowledgments

THIS BOOK WOULD NOT have happened without the unfailing love and support my husband, Curt, has shown throughout the development of this work. His patience when the process was inconvenient and the extra effort of keeping the kiddos occupied was a wonderful gift during the life of this work.

I want to thank my parents, Kevin and Kathy, who started me in the direction of music at a young age. You encouraged me to pursue my passions even when the doctors told me it may be time to give up. It is that fighting spirit that helps me to continue through the worst of storms.

I cannot forget to thank my children. Their interruptions and hugs remind me that work is not always the most important on my to-do list.

I want to acknowledge the wonderful work of all of my professors over the years. Thank you to Christopher Arneson, PhD, whose ability to craft coursework in the most approachable and creative manner gives his students the ability to understand and put to use even the most complex concepts. Furthermore, a thank you for being available and willing to guide beyond the degree and for the process of moving this work from thesis to book. Thank you also to Professor Stephen Purdy, whose skills in the studio help to tune and train with grace, and who has an expert knowledge of the contemporary voice, for encouraging me to look further than the easy fruits and to the bigger apples in the tree. And bravo to Kathy Kessler Price, PhD, whose up-lifting spirit brings a calm to what can be a scary world of voice science.

I am grateful to the professionals who have spent more years than I in the worship arts and were willing to sit down with me during their busy weeks. Your time and insights were instrumental in developing this resource for the singers of the church: Matthew Cox, Scott Allen, Walter Brath, DWS, and Shawn Holtgren, PhD.

I would like to acknowledge with gratitude the relatively few pedagogues I reference within and the many others who are contributing to the vocal pedagogy world through research and discovery in the studio and lab. The sharing of this knowledge enriches the lives of singers everywhere and is a wonderful gift to us all.

And certainly, not least, a thank you to the many friends in my life, including Tawney, Amber, and Gessica. Your prayers, efforts in checking in, and offerings of verbal support were more cherished than you know. Additionally, unending thanks to Joann. Words do not exist to express the impact you have had on this one.

Introduction

FROM THE MULTI-THOUSAND-MEMBER CONGREGATION in the metropolis to the one-hundred-member country church on the hillside of the small town, singers and their bandmates lead people in praise to God every week. Contemporary worship music has reached all over the earth and is presented in churches of all sizes and musicians of varying skill levels. In Ps 100:1, we are all called to "shout with joy to the Lord, all the earth!"—your skill level is not important. Yet God's people are also encouraged to "work enthusiastically for the Lord, for you know that nothing you do for the Lord is ever useless" (1 Cor 15:58). This book is built on the idea that those who are tasked with leading through song would not only benefit from but also be spiritually enriched by further training in their area of service. Then, this can also be passed on to the congregants who are inspired to greater faith by their work.

The church is made up of people from all different walks of life, and consequently, different backgrounds in vocal training, if any. There is the trained contemporary singer, the experienced classical and choral singer (I put these into the same category as the technique is similar when engaging in our discussion), as well as the non-trained/self-taught. I am writing to inform those who would like to further their understanding of the voice no matter what the starting point in vocal study may be. From the classically trained college graduate to the self-taught church volunteer and all those who fall on the very large spectrum in between.

WHY SHOULD I?

In the Old Testament, entering into the presence of God was not for just any casual believer. Only the holiest of men were permitted this honor. It was certainly an exclusive experience. Since Christ's death, we have all been granted the privilege to see our Lord right where we are. Yet, the charge of guiding others into the presence of the Almighty is not one to be looked upon lightly.

> The responsibility of singing in the church goes beyond the vocal task or simply standing on stage and singing with the congregation. Using the voice to lead the congregation in the time-honored practice of Christian worship, regardless of the worship style and form, invokes a responsibility to develop the singer's instrument, the voice.[1]

Does this mean that only the most talented musicians and voices, or perhaps the most faithful follower, should be allowed on the platform? Thankfully, no. We all know that if that were the case, the leadership position would be perpetually vacant. We all fall short of his glory. So, if God does not require perfection, why bother to improve anything, including your voice? What is the point in fretting over good breathing technique, specific vowel production, or even the longevity of our vocal health? Besides, God loves me where I am, he doesn't care about the quality of my voice.

Correct, God loves you as you are. And your congregation may not expect any more from you than what you already

1. Robinson, "Contemporary Worship Singers," 231.

give. However, God has created you for more. Vocal health and longevity aside, forget the aesthetically pleasing sound that you could make, think about how deep you could enter into God's presence when all possible distractions are removed, including the vocal ones. Now, imagine being this deep in worship personally while leading others. This is the ultimate goal behind improving your vocal skills, your gift. When you have polished your craft to a point that you do not need to worry about that one note, making it through that one phrase without running out of air, or even recalling that you may not have a voice at the end of the day; then your mind is free to focus on the sole purpose of the song.

God has given us every good thing, and just like a child does his best to make a gift for the parent probably being aware that it is not perfect, it is the work of giving God our finest. The quality of the gift is not what the parent values but knowing that the child has given his best in this act of love. For the singer and worship leader, giving our best means sharpening our skills to the greatest of our ability and presenting them with a joyful heart.

On a more practical note, music is an ever-changing language. The music styles that were prominent and popular forty years ago are not what is heard and employed at large today. Likewise, the music of the years to come will have changed from what we connect most with in the present. By training across styles, creativity blossoms, and the musician becomes more versatile and adaptable. The classical artist can learn from contemporary techniques, gospel artists can discover new methods from the jazz musician, and the contemporary artist can be enriched through the systems of the classical style.

HOW TO USE THIS BOOK

The purpose of this book is to provide the singer of contemporary worship music (CWM) with the tools to enhance vocal health, technique, and style. You will find an overview of the makeup of the vocal mechanism and guidelines for using it both healthily and in the CWM style. Take your time through the beginning sections and get to know the pieces and parts of the voice and how they work. This effort will enhance your understanding in later sections that discuss the nuances of the CWM style and stylistic differences between CWM and other styles of music.

A discussion of the vocal style of CWM will support the musical nuances vocalists should be considering. Along with these descriptions, you will find exercises to help the vocalist achieve the stylistic goals through healthy means. Use these exercises to test your skills and improve your technique to allow for a beneficial, free, and aesthetically appealing sound.

I will also mention a few common health matters as they relate to the voice. Singing can most certainly be a lifelong activity when the instrument is cared for. Knowing when to rest and when to strengthen through practice can help elongate the lifespan of your voice, and therefore, its ability to participate in that form of worship. If the voice is used correctly, you are more likely to avoid injuries that may result in being sidelined in addition to general frustration.

|

Parts of the Voice

THE VOICE IS AN intricate system, with many malleable parts, all working together to create each singer's sound. All instruments have three components. The generator, which provides the power, the singer's breath. The vibrator, which creates the sound, is the singer's voice box (larynx). Finally, the resonator, which helps to make the sound audible, shapes and colors the sound. This is the singer's vocal tract; the pathway through the throat, mouth, and nose that directs the sound out of the body to the people.

BREATHING SYSTEM

The air we use is the power source of the voice. It is how we talk, cough, sigh, and sing. In its most simple format, it is a two-step process where the lungs first expand to bring air into the body (inhalation) and the air flowing out (combined with the vocal folds coming together) causes vibrations in the vocal folds (exhalation) to form sound. Each one of these actions has its own set of muscles, the inspiratory (for inhaling) and the expiratory (for exhaling).

When discussing the breathing muscles in singing, the muscle that tends to get the most attention is the diaphragm. Here is a breakdown of what the diaphragm actually does. The muscle is at its resting point when the body is exhaling. This is when it simply sits just below the lungs in a dome shape. When it is time to inhale, the diaphragm expands in a downward motion, enlarging the lungs and pushing down on the organs below. As this action occurs, the lungs increase in size, and the air rushes into the open space.[1] This is where the job of the diaphragm is complete. It relaxes, shrinks, and returns to its resting position until the next inhale. Take note that the diaphragm only has one job: to help the lungs expand. Once the air has rushed in, this muscle gets to relax. The diaphragm does not help you sing. Singing occurs while the air is being released from the lungs. That is the job of other muscle groups, to be discussed shortly. So, if you never understood the phrase "sing with your diaphragm" you may now rest easier. It doesn't make sense anyway.[2] The diaphragm has no part in controlling the release of air.

1. Boyle's law (the concept that gases like to be in a state of equilibrium or evenness) plays a big role in the breathing process. Gases will always move from an area of high pressure to low pressure to find balance. With this in mind, know that all that is needed for a human to take in the air is for the lungs to get larger (this may be an oversimplification of the entire process, but it is the foundation of the course). It is attached to the lungs via the pleural sacs. When it is time to inhale, the diaphragm expands in a downward motion, enlarging the lungs and pushing down the organs below. As this action occurs, the lungs get larger, and the air rushes into the void of low pressure.

2. Miller, *Structure of Singing*, 20–25.

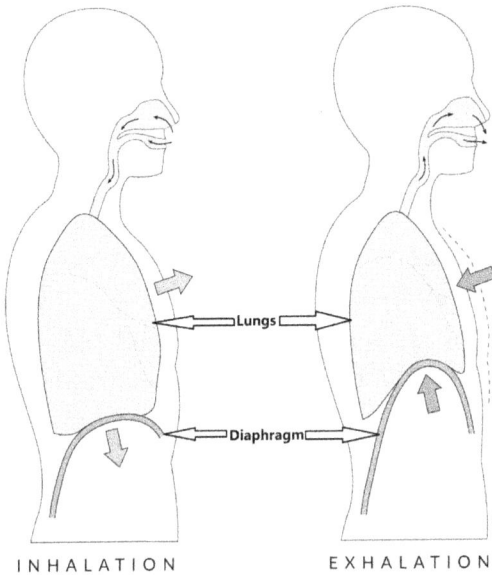

INHALATION   EXHALATION

The diaphragm does not work completely alone during inspiration. It has help from other inspiratory muscles to expand the space of the lungs, the external intercostal muscles. These muscles run in between the ribs and assist in their expansion. When the lungs require more space, the ribs expand due to these muscles being activated. And just like the diaphragm, their job ends here.

Once the inhale is complete, muscles that help control the speed at which air is released take over. These are called the expiratory muscles, and there are several of them: the internal intercostal muscles (which run in opposition to the internal intercostals), the rectus and transverse abdominis muscles, and the external oblique muscles. These muscles work to control the speed at which the air leaves the body to help the lungs stay open for the desired amount of time. If these muscles did not engage, the lungs would collapse quickly and all air would rush out. If the lungs are compressed at a slower rate, the air is released at a slower rate and the body can use the air more efficiently. So, maintaining the expanded space in the abdomen and chest is important.

Controlling the speed at which the air is released is imperative to controlling the volume, pitch, and length of a note. For the average healthy adult, it is even possible to build up more air pressure than the vocal folds can physically restrain. This can be harmful to the delicate vocal folds that are used to create sound. Therefore, the use of these muscles to control the air pressure is important so that vocal folds can focus on vibrating and creating the desired pitch rather than mitigating excess air pressure.

LARYNX

The voice box, Adam's apple, or, more technically, the larynx is where vocal folds[3] are located. Here the vibrations that create sound, and ultimately pitch, originate. This part of the body is a sophisticated mechanism made of cartilage, muscle, and other soft tissue. It is located at the topmost section of the trachea (or windpipe) and is also one of over fifty sphincters within the human body (a sphincter is a valve in the body that prevents matter from moving from one section to another[4]). In the case of the larynx, it functions as a valve for airflow as well as a barrier to prevent matter that is intended to be in the stomach from entering the lungs.

The larynx is a fairly small mechanism, approximately the size of a medium grape. The vocal folds themselves are another intricate facet of the supremely complicated human body.[5]

---

3. I refer to them as vocal folds rather than chords because they are more structured like flaps of tissue rather than stringlike strips.

4. "Sphincter muscle."

5. They are a fleshy tissue that has five different layers, each layer being more firm than the previous, from the most inward working out (I like to relate this to a chocolate layered lasagna desert with the soft whipped cream on top,

When the body is in a passive breathing position, the folds are separated to allow air to flow freely (abduction). These soft outer edges, supported by the more firm inner layers, come together in a V-shape to make sound or simply to hold back air (adduction). We experience this when we bear down to lift a heavy object.

Furthermore, the larynx is a movable device in the body. The height of the larynx has a direct effect on the color of the sound produced. The lower the larynx sits, the longer the vocal tract will be and the more time and space the sound waves have before exiting the body. This extra space aids in producing a fuller-bodied, legit or classical-type sound. Conversely, the higher the larynx rises, the less time the vibrations from the vocal folds have to be shaped before exiting. The smaller space produces a more pointed, conversational sound quality. It is possible to observe the movement of the larynx by noticing the motion of the voice box during a swallow or a yawn.

Gently place a few fingers on the front of your neck. Let out a yawn and notice the direction you feel the cartilage move. You will notice the larynx moving downward. To feel it move in the opposite direction, you can place your fingers gently in the same position and swallow. This demonstrates the larynx moving upward. Over time you can condition the body to have general control of the direction of movement for the larynx as well as take note of the effects it has on the color of the sound.

The vocal folds are controlled by two pairs of muscles, the thyroarytenoid muscles (TA) and the cricothyroid muscles (CT). Knowing these terms will help when discussing since the

---

then the gradually thicker mousse, fudge, and firm crust as the deepest layer). Though each of these layers is connected to the adjacent layer, they do act slightly independently. Take this chocolate dessert. If you were to jiggle the plate that holds the dessert you would notice that each layer moves slightly differently than the ones around it, yet they are all still one connected unit. Likewise, each layer of the vocal folds moves at different rates of motion.

type and pitch of sound produced, or registration, is defined by the muscles that are dominating control. The TA muscles are leading control when the vocal folds are thicker and more slack. They enable the voice to produce lower and louder pitches. The CT muscles are guiding control when the vocal folds are thinner, longer, and a bit tighter. The pitches produced are higher since the vibrations are happening at a faster rate and less of the folds are connecting.

It is important to know that though the vocal folds determine the pitch produced, the sound that the listener hears is not simply the result of the vocal fold's vibrations. If the singer were to remove the rest of the vocal tract (the pathway from the vocal folds to the outside world), the sound emanating from the vocal folds alone would amount to nothing more than a slight buzz. It would be difficult to distinguish one buzz from any other human's slight buzzing vocal folds. Each person's distinct sound is a result of not just the vibrations of the vocal folds, but also the pathway created by the structure leading from the larynx to the exit ramp of the mouth (vocal tract).

THROAT AND HEAD

The area above the larynx is called the pharynx. The pharynx is divided into three sections: the laryngeal pharynx (throat), the oral pharynx (open space behind the mouth), and the nasal pharynx (sinus area). In this area the sound waves bounce around, get louder, and take on more colorful tones. We call this the area of resonance. Scott McCoy describes resonance as that which "makes instruments louder and more beautiful by reinforcing the original vibrations of the sound source."[6]

There are two types of resonance: forced and free. A forced resonance occurs when the vibrations cause a solid mass to

---

6. McCoy, *Your Voice: An Inside View*, 22.

move or vibrate. In this instance, the vibrations are dampened and not allowed to grow. You can experience this phenomenon by noticing the vibrations in the chest when singing a low note. Free resonance is what happens when sound moves through an open space, unobstructed. The sound is then allowed to grow as it bounces off the sides of the space. This occurs in the vocal tract of the singer. The sound is bouncing around, enhancing, or dampening other sound waves, or echoes, as they interact with each other. If you can manipulate (or tune) the shape of the vocal tract in such a way as to direct some of the subsequent sound waves to arrive back at the glottis (the open space between the vocal folds) at the precise time that an initial sound wave is created, the intensity of the sound waves are boosted. This interaction is what allows classical singers to produce enough sound to sing over the powerful orchestra in the pit.

Resonance performs two jobs for our voice: it amplifies as well as colors the sound. We have mechanisms within the vocal tract to help direct where the sound waves bounce, reflect, and expand. Directing these sound waves to one area of the mouth by moving the tongue will produce one color of sound, while guiding the sound to another area by moving the soft palate (the soft, squishy area in the far back top of your mouth) will produce another color of sound. The number of ways to manipulate the sound waves are abundant. Some are efficient, requiring little effort and producing beautiful tones, while others restrict the sound, cause unnecessary tension, and can even fatigue or damage the vocal mechanism. Jeanette L. Lovetri states that "the vocal tract . . . is an almost infinitely variable tube capable of multitudes of resonance possibilities."[7] Some of the elements of our anatomy that assist in this tuning are the soft palate (velum), tongue, and the position of the larynx.

7. Lovetri, "Contemporary Commercial Music," 249.

The soft palate (velum) plays a role in both the digestive tract and the respiratory tract. It works to close off the passage between the mouth and the nasal cavity when one is needed over the other (think of swallowing or breathing through your nose). It also participates in directing the resonance of sound. When the singer is looking for a taller, more open sound, the soft pallet is raised and blocks most of the sound from entering the nasal cavity. When a more brassy, nasal sound is desired, the soft pallet can lower at varying degrees to help regulate the amount of sound entering and resonating in the nasal cavity. A very nasal sound has the soft palate in its lowest position allowing for the brightest, most stringent sound possible. The diagram below is a visual of what is mechanically occurring. The image on the left shows a closed mouth and lowered soft palate, only allowing air flow through the nose. This position is generally healthy for the mouth and tongue when you are not eating or communicating verbally. The image on the right indicates a raised soft palate, blocking the nasal cavity, just like when you are swallowing food. The image in the center depicts the soft palate in a middle position, which allows are to flow through both the nasal and oral cavities.

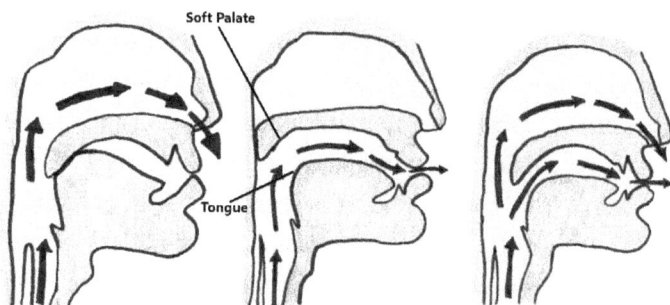

JAW

Let's focus on the jaw for a moment. This stabilizing structure for the mouth can be a source of many headaches (figuratively or literally) for the singer. It is also a vital component of the vocal tract, helping with tone color and communication. This body part, of course, is also important to the digestive process (chewing food). For singing, however, the jaw is best left relaxed. Jaw movement is not necessary for changes of pitch or vibrato (despite what you may have observed from other singers); it is only necessary for the shaping of some consonant sounds.

Jaw tension is relatively common and should be checked by all singers. The muscles that close the jaw are strong, as they are used throughout the day as a first step in the digestive process. The muscles that open the jaw are fewer and used less. The closing muscles can get very tight and overbearing if you do not check on them from time to time. Indications of jaw tension are pain in the jaw joint; using a mirror, observe if your jaw opens straight down or off to one side; checking the ease of pulsing the jaw; or taking stock to see if your jaw moves due to changes in pitch rather than changes in lyrics.

Noting the state of your jaw is good practice for any singer. Should you feel a consistent clicking or popping when opening, it is not a bad idea to bring it to the attention of your doctor or dentist at your next visit. There may even be a specialist in your area who can help ensure the alignment of the jaw joint (temporomandibular joint) is correct. Addressing jaw discomfort may not only affect your singing but overall discomfort in the ear and head as well.

ARTICULATORS

The articulators are what turn our unintelligible sounds into words. They include the mouth, the lips, and the tongue. It is with these elements that we produce vowels and consonants. Vowels are produced with zero obstruction to the airflow, while consonants are produced with some resistance to the flow of air. There are also sounds that fall in the middle of this spectrum called semivowels, and despite their name, they are usually classified with the consonants as they are produced in a similar manner.[8]

The position of the tongue determines which vowels are produced. Because vowels are created using free-flowing air and sound waves, the tongue is simply directing and helping to shape these sound waves. Dinesh Ramoo suggests that we can define vowels by the lateral and vertical placement (*backness*) within the mouth. *Height* refers to the vertical position the tongue takes during phonation. If you were to alternate between an *ee* [i] and an *ah* [a] vowel (similar to the *hee-haw* sound a donkey makes) they could get an idea of the feeling of the height the tongue may or may not achieve when producing a vowel. The *backness* can be determined by looking at the placement of the tongue on a lateral scale. You can determine this feeling by alternating between *ee* [i] and *oo* [u]. In the first vowel, the tongue sits more toward the front of the mouth while the second falls more toward the back. The tongue also contributes to our resonance. The tongue is a complex muscle made of eight smaller pairs of muscles. The part that we are most familiar with is the dorsum or the blade of the tongue. The root is attached to the floor of the mouth and the hyoid bone, from which the larynx is suspended.[9] The other portions

---

8. Ramoo, *Psychology of Language*, 31.

9. Hyoid bone—this is a very small piece of bone that is one of only three bones in your body not connected to any other bones (the other two are your

of the tongue work to shape and move it into the precise position needed for the sound that our brain is working to produce. Just as it takes a young child years to maneuver the spoken language, it also takes the singer time and effort to fine-tune the ability to produce the sound desired.

Due to the large nature of the tongue, it is easy to see how it can be a helpful or obstructive entity within the vocal tract. Should the tongue rise too high in the mouth, it can block the flow of sound and air on its way out. If the tongue were to be pushed too low, it could block the flow in the throat due to the root being attached to that region. Richard Miller categorizes the tongue as "the ringleader in determining the resonator-tube shape."[10] Therefore, it is important to keep the tongue relatively relaxed and in a rather forward position within the mouth while singing. Trineice Robinson-Martin speaks to the difficulty singers have regarding the tongue. It is essential for the singer to learn to control the amount of tension the tongue produces especially in the unseen area, the back of the tongue.[11] When singing, a home base position is to have the tongue resting on the bottom of the mouth, just behind the front teeth.

When it seems as though the tongue is spending too much time toward the back of the mouth feel free to stick it out. Let your tongue hang as far out of your mouth as possible while singing through a phrase or two. Put the lyrics to the side for this exercise. Just sing the pitches on an *ah* [a]. This will help to release a bit of tension in the back region of the muscle as well

---

kneecaps or patellae). That is to say, the only thing holding the hyoid bone in place is soft tissue. This bone helps in three different functions of the mouth. It is connected to the upper pull of the larynx, the root of the tongue, and the spot where the muscles that open the lower jaw live. The connections of this bone are why tension in the tongue can also lead to tension in other areas of the mouth.

10. Miller, *On the Art of Singing*, 228.

11. Benson and Blades, *Training Contemporary Commercial Singers*, 92.

as assist in making you more aware of the feeling of the tongue resting more towards the front of the mouth.

Another way to improve awareness of the tongue is to mouth through a song. Shape the lyrics as if you were singing them, but do not make a sound. Pay attention to where your tongue is throughout the phrase. By isolating the lyrics from the nature of singing, you are giving your brain the chance to focus more on the task of forming the lyrics. You will have the ability to notice tongue movements that are excessive more easily than during singing.

The position of the larynx also affects the sound that is produced. A lowered, stable larynx (one that does not move with the changing of pitches) creates a longer distance for the sound to travel. The result (when coupled with a more open space in the rest of the vocal tract) can be a more full, rounded sound. Miller explicitly states that this is the "universal mark of good singing" in the classical world.[12] When the larynx is in a higher position, the resulting sound tends to be of a brighter quality.[13] In general, when the vocal tract gives less space for the sound to reverberate, the result is a sharper, slightly thinner, and more stringent sound.[14]

In addition, the position of the lips helps to determine the sound of a vowel. When they are the farthest apart vertically, with minimal spread in the width, you will produce an *ah* [a] sound. While the closest position of the lips, similar to pursed lips (without being completely closed) will produce an *oo* [u] vowel. The other vowels fall somewhere between these two extremes with varying degrees of lateral and vertical spread. Understanding how these sounds are created can help the singer evaluate the efficiency of their.

12. Miller, *On the Art of Singing*, 229.

13. Lovetri, "Contemporary Commercial Music."

14. Saldías et al., "Vocal Tract."

The same can be said of the consonants. The explanation of these is much more complex, as they number many more than the thirteen vowel sounds heard in the English language. The basic concept is that by bringing any of the articulators together to restrict the airflow you can achieve the consonant sounds. Connecting the back of the top teeth and the end of the tongue, combined with a light puff of air will give you a *t* [t] sound. Pressing the lips together and releasing in a puff of air will produce a *p* [p] sound, while gently touching them together and phonating will give you a hmm [m] sound. Humans use many different combinations of these articulators as the mouth is a complex cavity.

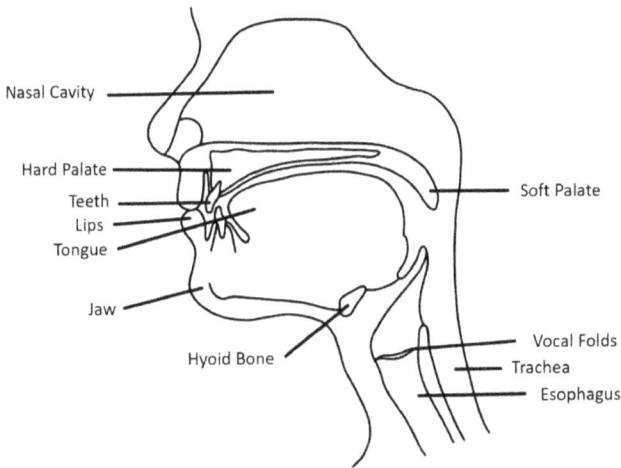

Though the anatomy of the voice can be a bit confusing, overwhelming, or off-putting at first, having an overall knowledge of the different body parts and their functions serves the vocalist in numerous ways. If nothing else, it assists the singer in being more self-aware of the feelings experienced during singing. This awareness can help to identify strengths to build on and points of weakness when evaluating the singer's technique, consequently accelerating the process of improvement.

2

CWM Style Is . . .

HAVING A COMMON KNOWLEDGE of the style that a musician is working to achieve can help guide the singer in multiple ways. It informs the type of technique that will be used and helps to make a cohesive-sounding ensemble/band. It gives parameters of customary sounds, as well as a guide when looking to expand the level of expression within the style. Perhaps the most important, it helps to eliminate potential distractions for the congregation that may arise from disjunction in style between band members.

CWM style is very similar to other contemporary styles of our time in a few ways. A listener can hear in it elements of pop music, folk, rock as well as jazz, and gospel. Of course, the main difference between CWM and other genres of music is the subject. CWM is about God and his relationship with us. Other, less important vocal stylistic characteristics come from the placement of the tone, the registration, the way emotion is expressed, the use of embellishments, and even the way the breath is utilized. Let's walk through these stylistic elements.

TALKY/FORWARD

In contemporary music, the singer should be aware that the lyrics are crucial and need to be understood by the listener. To lead others into the presence of Christ and to help them praise the one the song is about, they need to understand the words they are being asked to recite. Because of this need for clarity, the singer needs to have a conversational and speechlike approach to the lyrics, with an emphasis on consonants.

This orientation towards speech, combined with the assistance of electronic amplification, gives the singer freedom to explore many different vocal sounds and colors. It gives the singer the ability to use a brighter, forward, focused, and clear tone since they do not have to rely on the body to be the sole producer of sound magnification. This also allows CWM music to be speechlike and conversational; therefore the consonants are often given equal weight, as they would in everyday speech.

As discussed in the anatomy section, Lovetri mentions that brighter sounds have a smaller space in the vocal tract.[1] We discussed how the body can make spaces within the vocal tract smaller by raising the larynx slightly or adjusting the articulators within the mouth. But what does this sound like when singing? Here are a few exercises that can help you work on this technique.

Think of a naughty child taunting another. For this exercise, we want the annoying, bothersome sound to assist in locating some of the nasal quality that should be added to CWM tone. The higher-pitched stringent sound comes quite easily when put in the right context. Male and female voices should start around B above middle C (B[4]) moving up four half steps, then coming back down to the starting note:

1. Lovetri, "Contemporary Commercial Music."

Nya Nya Nya Nya   Nya   Nya Nya Nya Nya   Nya

Begin with the vowel sounds *ee* [i] and *oo* [u]. Feel free to add some consonant sounds for variety and to the initiation of the sound such as *t* [t] or *d* [d]. This exercise should start in the middle of your range; for ladies a G above middle C (G⁴) and for guys a G below middle C (G³). Move up by half steps about five times, then by half steps move back down to the starting pitch:

Ee-oo-ee-oo - ee   Ee-oo-ee-oo - ee   Ee-oo-ee-oo - ee
Tee-oo-ee-oo - ee   -   -   -
Dee-oo-ee-oo - ee   -   -   -

Singing straight from *zoo* [zu] to *ee* [i], use this exercise to work on connecting the lower notes with the higher notes. After the *ee* [i] vowel is routinely forward, modify to a vowel that sits a bit further back on the tongue such as *ah* [a] or *oh* [o]. Begin in the chest voice (ladies around middle C (C⁴) and guys around the C below (C³) and work your way up into the middle voice, focusing on keeping the sound in the front of the mouth even as the pitches ascend:

Zoo - Ee   -
Zoo - Ah   -
Zoo - Oh   -

Once the singer has realized this brassy and clear tone in their singing, take note of how it feels. Practice recovering that same sound each day until it is effortless. Learning to access this more extreme tone gives the singer more flexibility in choosing the amount of nasality desired at any given moment in singing. It also gives the singer an easier path to cross when traveling from one register to another.

REGISTRATION

If you want to see an intense, heated, and passionate engagement between otherwise sophisticated and refined singing teachers, you can simply throw out the term *registration*. Go ahead, ask how many there are. What are they called? Do they vary between voice types? The opinions and facts will fly at lightning speed and with great conviction. Though the vocal pedagogy world has not yet come to a firm consensus on this matter, what I can tell you is that semantics should not get in the way of the physiological events of this topic. Many a voice teacher is working on defining the best labels for this subject matter and the task has proven quite challenging. For the intents and purposes of this discussion, I am going to stick to four registration moments in the contemporary voice, as well as give you some alternative titles for cross reference. I have chosen these terms because they are widely used, and the general concept has proven relatable for many singers. They are labeled the chest, mix, head, and falsetto registers.

The *chest register* (also called Mode I or TA dominant) refers to the lower group of notes that a person sings comfortably. Though the sound is not produced in the chest cavity (it is produced in the same location as every other sound the voice makes, the larynx), many singers perceive vibrations in the chest, hence the name for this register.[2]

Many wonder if it is ever harmful to use a full chest register. Near the bridge (passaggio, break) of your voice, it can be if any tension or heavy tone of the lower notes is used. (This bridge area is the point in your voice when the vocal folds are getting less reliant on one muscle pair and more reliant on the other. You are moving from the head to the chest register or vice versa.) As you move towards higher notes, from the thick, more relaxed state of the chest voice to the thinner and more stretched state of the head voice, you will want to *mix* your sound. You can do this by balancing the muscle use of the two registers.[3] By attempting to bring the chest register up too high, the results will be a strained sound, less control of volume and pitch, as well as the increased possibility for damage (short or long term) to the voice itself. Using the chest register with too high of pitches will result in more effortful singing and is much less efficient.

To identify your chest register, begin first by speaking *ah* [a]. This could be similar to when someone has just explained a concept you found difficult to understand. Now, turn that spoken *ah* [a] into a sung *ah* [a] in a comfortable low register. Ladies may begin around middle C (C^4) and guys around the E (E^3) or F (F^3) below. Be gentle and do not give a lot of weight to these notes. They carry very well on their own:

2. Miller, *Structure of Singing*, 115.

3. Note: technically, the voice is always using both sets of muscles no matter the note. The chest voice is simply using the TA muscles more than the CT muscles and the head voice is using the CT muscles more than the TA muscles. When mentioning the "mix" voice, I am referring to using both muscle sets in a more equal ratio.

Ah - - -
Mee - - -

Sing a descending 5-note scale with the top note being toward the top of the chest voice and working downward on a *yah* [ia]. As descending keep the tone gentle and do not push with any muscles downward.

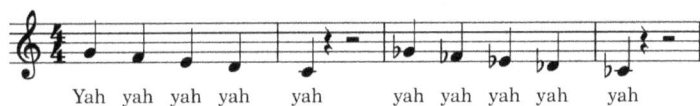

Yah yah yah yah   yah   yah yah yah yah   yah

Sing a three-note scale on *uh* [ʌ] [open-mid vowel sound, upside down [v] as if starting an old engine in cold weather. Ladies start around B (B^3) below middle C, guys around E (E^3) below middle C. Descend by half steps. Volume is not the main goal, but rather the fullness of sound.

Uh uh uh uh   uh   Uh uh uh uh   uh

The next two registers *falsetto* and *head register* can be a bit confusing as these terms are often used interchangeably. However, there is a physiological distinction that can be made between the two. Falsetto and head register (Mode II, CT dominant) are the higher registers of the voice. They are used less frequently than their lower counterparts in contemporary singing. The biggest difference between falsetto and head voice is the tone quality. The falsetto tone is a lighter, breathier sound caused by a slight separation of the vocal folds at one end where air escapes.[4]

The head register is a more full-bodied sound since the entire length of the vocal folds comes in contact with each other. More air pressure is present compared to falsetto, and more sound is produced. In contemporary music, both registers are used occasionally, according to the sound and effect the artist desires to communicate.

Despite these registers being utilized less frequently in contemporary styles, I advise the contemporary vocalist to work on developing this register of the voice nonetheless. Many songs use this register to some degree. A singer may never know when he may be called upon to lead during one of these songs. The singer has much versatility to be gained by developing this register of the voice. Having that tool in your belt and ready to step up can mean the difference between a smooth Sunday morning or one with avoidable anxiety. Additionally, developing this head register certainly gives you options when it comes to presenting a song. It is also true that the head register, though employed infrequently on its own, is an essential component of the mixed voice. You cannot have a functioning mixed voice without having the head to *mix* with the chest (more on this to come soon).

> A gentle sigh is a great way to help locate a head voice that seems to be hiding. Start on a very light, high pitch as if just settling in after a long day.

---

4. Miller, *Structure of Singing*, 120.

You can also use what is referred to as a siren in the vocal world. It begins on a low pitch and slides into the upper register and then back down. Much like you may hear from an emergency vehicle (between the short, piercing, loud whoops).

The exercise below should begin in the head register, around a C above middle C (C^5) for ladies and an E (E^4) above middle C for guys. This can be done in two different manners. A quick, light staccato (notes sung very shortly) is a good way to begin. Once you've gained some comfort in this area, smoothing out the notes and connecting them will help to improve your control of the pitch.

Nee-ah-ee-ah-ee-ah-ee-ah - oo   Nee-ah-ee-ah-ee-ah-ee-ah - oo

Employing the *mixed* voice in the CWM style is highly useful. The tricky part about this range of notes is that the chest voice and the head are often capable of producing the pitches on their own, but the further you sing on the edges of these registers, the less control you have over the pitches and the more difficult it is to have a smooth transition to another register. As the TA muscles are used to being dominant in the chest voice and the CT muscles are used to being dominant in the head voice, this middle ground gives way to a bit of a power struggle. When the voice does not take a balanced approach to the disbursement of power in this range of notes, the singer ends up with one set of muscles dominating and a terribly clunky handoff.

Think of it this way: in a relay race the athletes are required to pass off the baton when their section of track has been run. This skill takes time to perfect between teammates to ensure that all goes smoothly. Just as one person's hand is reaching out to give, the others must be prepared to receive. If either athlete grabs too hard or resists the release of control, they are all likely to end up in a pile on the track floor. The athletes practice extending the hand, easing off the grip, or having an open hand ready to gently receive the package, all while coordinating the rest of the body to move, maintaining the team's position in the race. The handoff must be delicate and seamless amid all the commotion. The chest and head register need to do such work. Though the notes are ever-changing, rhythms may be challenging, and lyrics demand constant adjustments in the vocal tract, the muscles of the vocal folds need to learn to work together in a more balanced fashion through the range of notes where they are both capable of dominating control. This technique is not easy to learn but it is incredibly valuable and will be used in nearly every song in the CWM style.

> Use this exercise to get things moving. Slide between the bottom and top notes. Begin in the chest voice, around middle C (C⁴) for ladies and around E below middle C (E³) for guys and work your way up. Then invert the exercise and work the head voice into the mixed area for versatility.

Mm – mm – mm –
Moo – oo – oo –
Mee – ee – ee –
Mah – ah – ah –

The *oo* [u] vowel is good for crossing through the mixed voice. Begin in chest voice and move stepwise toward the mixed voice register. Take your time to produce each note accurately. Play around with adding forward consonants such as *n* [n] or *m* [m]. As the skill improves, the speed may also.

Oo   -   -   -
Noo   -   -   -

BELTING

A correct belt (or the call) is a commanding, boisterous, and emotionally charged sound that is not intrinsically harmful to the voice.[5] When produced in a healthy approach, the belt does not require pushing or excess tension in the throat at all. Instead, the air pressure and the shape of the vocal tract do the heavy lifting. The belt is not a register unto itself but is a sound quality that can occur across a broad spectrum of pitches. It is the manner in which the notes are delivered and not dependent on the register they fall into.

The belt quality often is a mixed sound (in reference to register).[6] Due to the general pitches the belt is usually used for, this tone is achieved by mixing the registers of the chest

5. I do find the term "call of the voice" helpful as it gives the singer a good concept as to what the sound should resemble. When one is quite literally calling out to another, the "call" or "belt" voice is naturally used. Since this is a natural state of the voice, it takes away from the mystery of the sound as well as helping to calm any nerves one may have of the register being inherently unhealthy.

6. Saunders-Barton and Spivey, *Cross Training*, 48.

and head. Dr. Norman Spivey explains, "Belt is not chest voice. If the chest voice is mistakenly used and carried up into the high range and is taught as Belt, the vocal instrument will be ruined."[7] Though nailing down a universal definition for the belt has proven elusive for the voice community, you can keep in mind that it is another speechlike quality that is more akin to a calling out. It is not a full chest sound and needs to be coupled with a forward placement to avoid unnecessary tension in the vocal mechanism.

> Try this: Call out as if your teammate is about to score for the other team. Or imagine you're riding in a car, and the driver is moving to turn the wrong way down a one-way street:
>
> *Hey, you're going the wrong way!*
>
> Think about a time when you found out the shocking news you couldn't believe was true:
>
> *No way!*
> *Oh my!*
>
> Now, try matching a pitch to the call you just produced. For ladies, it may be around G–B above middle C (G^5–B^5), and guys around F above middle C (F^4).

Oo –   –   –
Noo –   –   –

---

7. Spivey, "Music Theater Singing," 609.

No Way!   No Way!

EMOTIONAL

CWM can also be characterized by the emotional content it exhibits. Some songs are joyful and elicit clapping hands and shouts of joy. Other songs are more subdued and prompt a more introspective response. The spectrum is wide, and the emotions fall on every point in this line. The vocal style of the singer needs to also reflect the emotional context of the lyrics. This is achieved by the aforementioned vocal registers as well as other characteristic sounds the voice is capable of creating. The sounds and colors mentioned below are tools the singer can use to show off these emotions.

ONSET AND OFFSET

The term *onset* refers to how the vocal folds and the airflow interact when starting the sound. We can divide this sound into three types of onsets: the aspirated onset, the even onset, and the glottal attack.

The aspirated onset is an initial sound that begins with some air before the pitch sounds. It gives a breathy sense to the notes and lyrics. This can be heard any time there is a start of a new sound (often at the beginning of a phrase or sometimes in the middle of a phrase that has breaks within it) but is often heard with the consonant *h* [h] (this *h* is often added to the front of a word beginning with a vowel such as *oh* in open). It can add extra color to the piece that cannot otherwise be conveyed with sound or even consonants. A breathy onset can be heard in the song "10,000 Reasons" with the phrase "oh my soul" as well as "Who You Say I Am" with the phrase "who the son."[8] However, this type of onset can be taxing on the delicate vocal folds. Leon Neto reminds the singer that though breathiness is not intrinsically bad for the voice, several expert vocal teachers of the past have noted that "the prolonged use of this type of phonation can have a negative impact on the laryngeal mechanism."[9]

It is wise to keep in mind that breathiness is not uncommon for the male voice often in the lower part of their ranges and for the female voice in the upper section of their range. It is likely that this breathiness is a result of inefficient sound production and tends to improve as the technique of the singer improves.[10] This breathiness is slightly different from the breathy onset (in that is it sustained throughout a melodic line).

The glottal attack (which is slightly different from the glottal onset that occurs naturally in English and causes no harm to the voice when done gently[11]) is that little *click* or grab you may hear just before a note sounds. It occurs when the vocal folds come together (in a rather forceful manner) before air flows to create the vibrations that make the note. This type of sound initiation often occurs before a vowel. The sound tends to give intensity and even aggressiveness that the song may otherwise lack. This can be heard in the songs "House of the Lord," especially in the lyric "evermore," and "King of Kings" with the words "in your eyes."[12] You may also hear it frequently used in pop and rock music. This too is an onset that when used too often can result in vocal trauma. Neto notes that an alternative can be employed to limit the use of glottal attacks by using

8. Redman, "10,000 Reasons"; Hillsong Worship, "Who You Say I Am."

9. Neto, "Contemporary Christian Music," 197.

10. Neto, "Contemporary Christian Music."

11. Kathy Kessler-Price, email message to author, Nov 28, 2022.

12. Wickham, "House of the Lord"; Hillsong Worship, "King of Kings."

staccato rhythms for the initial note if the singer is struggling to limit those glottal attacks.[13]

An even onset exists when the vocal folds come together just as the air pressure is sufficient to produce the desired pitch. The vocal folds begin to sound in a gentle and timely manner. This type of initiation to the note is generally preferred because it puts the least amount of strain or pressure on the vocal folds.

Take this first one nice and slow. Allow for a bit of space between each note. Let the *mm* [m] sound help to initiate the vowel and use the next four notes to practice an even onset without the help of the consonant. Take your time at first. Give your brain time to process the sound it is looking for and how to make it. When the exercise gets easier, then the tempo can increase. Start on a comfortable note in your chest range. Ladies can start around an E (E⁴) above middle C and guys can start around F (F³) below middle C.

Me - ee - ee - ee - ee   Me - ee - ee - ee - ee
Mo - oh - oh - oh - oh   Mo - oh - oh - oh - oh

Now that you have worked on initiating the vowel sound, it is time to change pitches with your even onset. Again, starting in the chest range. Ladies can start around an E (E⁴) above middle C and guys can start around F (F³) below middle C.

13. Neto, "Contemporary Christian Music," 197.

ee - eh - ah - oh - oo   ee - eh - ah - oh - oo

Know that it is not harmful to use the other onsets in moderation. Many singers, in many different genres of music, have been using these variations in sound for years without damage to the vocal mechanism. The key is to use them intentionally for effect rather than to sing this way out of habit.[14] If you struggle to break the habit of using aspirated or glottal onsets, other vocal distortions, or even have difficulty producing an even onset, it is a good idea to consult a voice professional.

AMPLIFICATION

It is no secret that a characteristic of CWM is the use of amplification. Though there may be the occasional small group setting where an acoustic set is employed, the majority of the time this music is used in larger venues where microphones and speakers are required. These tools allow the singer to use the stylistic nuances of contemporary music, such as a breathy tone, twangy placement, or speech quality. The amplification system is able to take the softer, more gentle, and percussive sounds and make them heard by the audience. This way, the singer no longer has the burden of ensuring they are loud enough to be heard; they can focus fully on communicating the music.

Knowing how to use your microphone allows this tool to be the most beneficial. The microphone can be a great device for communication, or it can be a hindrance if not managed correctly. Everything from the angle of the microphone to the

14. OfficialNATS, "Contemporary Vocal Styles."

distance it is from your mouth, or correct hand placement, is important to the function of the microphone.[15] For example, holding the microphone too far away or at the wrong angle keeps it from picking up the full depth of the sounds created, causing the singer to compensate by singing louder, often beyond what is comfortable or healthy. The microphone is there to assist your voice so, do not fight it. Speak with the sound technician regarding the best way to use the equipment that is provided to optimize the features with which the microphone is equipped.

Monitors are another integral component of the amplification system that helps you to hear yourself and the other instruments, helping to prevent fatigue and possible vocal damage from oversinging. Monitors can be located in the surrounding area, like wedge monitors, or they can be an earbud-type configuration (also known as *in ears*); both forms have benefits.

A wedge monitor is more cost-effective. It requires less supportive equipment and can service more than one musician at a time (assuming they have similar needs in the audio feedback). The in-ear monitor system can be tailored more to the individual demands of each musician. Neto also notes that "this system can offer great mobility and give more control capabilities to the singer."[16] Additionally in-ears can provide some protection to hearing function as it helps to block out uncontrolled sounds that may rise above desirable levels. However, it is good to note that any monitor turned up too loud can damage your hearing no matter the delivery method.[17]

15. OfficialNATS, "Contemporary Vocal Styles."
16. Neto, "Contemporary Christian Music," 198.
17. Blum, "Music to Their Ears," para. 25.

EMBELLISHMENTS

CWM music uses different types of runs and ad-libs within the melody to convey various emotional states within a song. Though these embellishments are not employed very often, and usually only by the lead vocalist, they are present and most often during instrumental sections of songs. These ad-libs can be heard quite clearly in the live recorded version of "Grave into Gardens."[18] To truly be in the CWM style, Neto advises "not to overuse embellishments and to vary the melody with simplicity and good taste."[19] The singer needs to be aware that the congregation is following your lead spiritually and melodically. If the embellishments occur too frequently or make the melody difficult to discern, the leader runs the risk of losing the participation of congregants. It is also important to remember that, while you may be singing from an emotional or spiritual spot, getting too technical or flashy with the agility of your instrument could be perceived as the singer performing for the people rather than worshiping God. Unlike other genres that employ the use of ad-libs, the purpose in CWM music is to communicate the overflow of your heart, prayer, and communication with God. Do not feel pressured to make this part of worship a show of your skill, but rather a display of the relationship you share with your Savior. While there are no real rules to follow in this area, the artist has freedom to let the Spirit and music guide their choices (what one person sees as flashy and over the top may inspire another to dig in deeper emotionally and spiritually). Use your best judgment; lean on your teammates and church leaders to discern how the congregation is responding and what may be appropriate.

18. Elevation Worship, "Graves into Gardens."
19. Neto, "Contemporary Christian Music," 198.

Scooping into the note is another way to add style to a melody. The number of notes that come before the intended melodic note can vary depending on the artist, but we are usually talking about adding a note a whole or half step below that intended melodic note (depending on the key of the song). These embellishments usually happen when there is a skip of a third or more in the melody. While this technique does not have any health concerns for the voice per say, you should still consider using this technique in moderation, as it helps to accentuate a thought or emotion in a song, and if it is overused you run the risk of losing the effect. The song "I Thank God" shows how well scooping can be employed.[20] You can hear scooping on the phrase "forever free" in the chorus, but it is not plentiful in the verses. You can also hear scooping in the song "His Mercy Is More" in the lyric "more."[21]

Falling off the end of phrases is also a characteristic of the CWM style. The term *falling off* references when a singer hits the intended note, usually at the end of a phrase, but then hits a few notes below the intended note before cutting off the lyric completely. You can hear this technique in the song "Who You Say I Am" the first couple of times the singer presents the word "me."[22]

Earlier I discussed some of the characteristics that make CWM singing more conversational and speechlike. While the consonants can be used for a more percussive sound, they can also be used for their voiced qualities such as harder r's [ɹ] and l's [l]. In "House of the Lord" you can hear the elongated l [l] in the word "place" as well as the accented r [ɹ] in the word "praise."[23] The accented r is also evident in one of the first recordings of

---

20. TRIBL, "I Thank God."

21. Papa and Boswell, "His Mercy Is More."

22. Hillsong Worship, "Who You Say I Am."

23. Wickham, "House of the Lord."

"How Deep the Father's Love for Us" on both the word "Father" and "for."[24]

VIBRATO

That quick-moving pitch oscillation that occurs on an extended note (in CWM it is usually at the end of a phrase) is called vibrato. Borch defines it as "rapid, repetitive variation in pitch."[25] Vibrato, in its natural state, is a result of the larynx being relaxed and the muscles that control the pitch (TA and CT muscles) being allowed to move in an unobstructed way. Vibrato is used in CWM as another color choice for the song. It tends to be introduced at the end of a phrase and is a way to warm a sound that could come across as a bit cold. Otherwise, an even or *straight* tone is generally desired in the CWM genre. One song that demonstrates both very well is "Thank You, Jesus, for the Blood" sung by Charity Gale.[26] If you listen to the ends of her phrases, you'll hear both a very straight tone that drops off the end, as well as a free, subtly present vibrato.

> A good exercise to help ensure relaxation in the voice while singing starts with puffy cheeks. Allow your cheeks to fill up with air and get nice and full. Be cautious not to let your lips press tightly together. They should be closed only gently.

> Next, allow a tiny bit of air to escape through the lips (place one finger in front of your lips to verify a slight bit of air is escaping).

24. Townend, "How Deep the Fathers Love."

25. Borch, *Ultimate Vocal Voyage*, 51.

26. Charity Gayle, "Thank You Jesus."

Finally, allow a pitch to sound. Try it in a register that gives you the most trouble/tension in singing. For some, it may be the chest area where they tend to struggle for volume. Others it may be the head voice where tension creeps in due to fear of those scary high notes. Some may choose the middle voice where the belt becomes more of a push.

Once the puffy cheeks have been employed, switch to a hum. Hum the note first, then open to an *ah*. Be careful not to change anything in your mouth. The only difference in producing the *ah* is the position of the jaw, let it fall open in a relaxed motion. Ladies start on E above middle C (C⁴), guys on E below middle C (C³). Slowly introduce larger intervals.

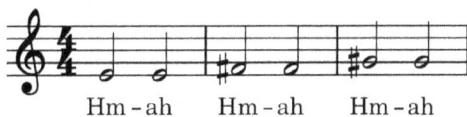

Hm - ah   Hm - ah   Hm - ah

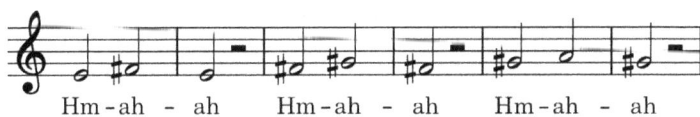

Hm - ah - ah   Hm - ah - ah   Hm - ah - ah

Use this method on your easiest or most challenging melody.

Next, progress from puffy cheeks to a hum on the same melodic line. Finally adding back in the lyrics. This will help to train the voice to relax.

CAUTION

So, now that you have learned different ways to make your sound more like the CWM style that you have been looking for. Why do you still feel like you're sticking out? Here are a few culprits that could be affecting your voice production.

Too nasal—maybe you are experiencing a sound that is very *nasal* or it lacks depth and body. While some people naturally have more nasal engagement in their voice it doesn't have to be overly present. If your sound is excessively nasal then you have an abundance of sound waves resonating in your nasal cavity rather than bouncing around in the mouth before the grand exit. Some of those sound waves need to be redirected away from the nasal area toward the mouth, where they have a little more space to play. The soft palate (the squishy part of the roof of your mouth) is the key. Here are a couple of exercises to help engage your conscious control of the soft palate.

Get your favorite (imaginary) milkshake in front of you. As you suck the extremely thick substance through the straw, take note of the action in the top back of your mouth. What you are feeling is your soft palate raising up to seal off the nasal passage. Suck in again and then open to an *ah* [a] vowel on a comfortable note. Go up by half steps, sucking in some milkshake before each *ah* [a]. Do not be surprised if you begin to yawn, things are working correctly.

Another way to work on your conscious control of the soft palate starts with a simple swallow. Take note of the feeling in the top of your mouth when you do so. This is your soft palate raising up. Swallow a few more times to enhance your awareness of this area. Then work to move that soft palate without the full swallowing action.

Too thin—do you sound a little too young for your age? Or is your sound too small and maybe a bit too stringent? You could use a little more space inside your mouth for the sound to bounce around, echo, and grow before exiting into the room. Though we are not looking for an extremely tall and operatic sound, a little space can make a big difference in the depth of your tone.

One thing to remember is to not let the corners of your mouth spread too wide. If a broader sound is what you are looking for, place the tips of your index fingers on the corners of your mouth. Go back and forth between an *ah* [a] and *ee* [i] on a comfortable note striving to keep the lips from spreading.

Too tall/lofty—do you sound more like an opera singer than a CWM singer? In this case, your sound may be quite efficient and acceptable for the classical music setting but stylistically incorrect for CWM. The overall solution for this is to aim to make your singing more like talking.

> You may achieve this by reading the lyrics to a song a time or two (similar to reading a story out loud). Then add the notes as if you are simply talking on pitch. Do not think about singing or working too hard on any other skill at this point, just tell the story on the pitches given. The goal here is to be relatable and conversational in your communication. This technique will help the tall open vowels to shrink down slightly and become a more contemporary sound.

Sore throat or hoarseness—as mentioned before, it is not normal or healthy for your throat or voice to be sore or hoarse every Sunday afternoon. Though there are many possible causes for this issue, one basic thing to check begins with the height of your voice box (larynx). Often when the chest voice is being used on notes higher than is healthy, the singer will know because the voice is tired and/or sore. There may even be a loss of higher pitches. Though the talky, strident sound of contemporary music is made with a shortened vocal tract, if the larynx (voice box) is pulled up too high, too often, the muscle fatigues and soreness ensue, and those high notes will not happen at all. Rubin, Mathieson, and Blake note that "a higher position of the larynx in the neck reduces the efficiency of the voice as we reach for higher notes and can ultimately cause a reduction in the upper part of the pitch range (how high we can sing)."[27] As always, a balance must be found.

---

27. Rubin et al., "Posture and Voice," 273.

To get a feeling for your voice box moving up and down, touch your larynx (or Adam's apple) and swallow once. Notice at the initial motion the voice box moves up. It is following the motion of the tongue. Then, take note of the downward motion that follows. Do this a few times to gain awareness of your control over the voice box. Next, yawn a few times. This is another moment where you can really feel the downward motion of the voice box.

Now sing on a *yah* [ia] syllable relaxed and gentle, as if you are tired and calm (be careful, this one may bring on a yawn or two). As the notes descend be aware of the relaxed state of the voice box. (Yes, we have used this exercise before, it is a good one.) Begin this exercise in the chest voice and work your way up. Ladies begin around G (G^4) above middle C, guys around F (F^3) below middle C.

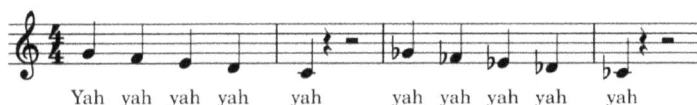

Yah yah yah yah   yah   yah yah yah yah   yah

Once you have done well with the previous exercise, work to keep everything relaxed as the notes ascend. Start with *yah* [ia] and play around with different syllables, making note of the more challenging choices.

Yah   -   -   Yah   -   -

Cracking on leaps—are your notes cracking or breaking when you are singing a leap or a larger interval? Like other issues, there can be multiple causes for this phenomenon, but it can occur due to inconsistent airflow. Just like a car will use less fuel by driving straight through town with all green lights, rather than having to stop at every intersection; the voice is more efficient when the airflow is consistent rather than stopping and starting from one note to the next. It is important that the generator is consistently providing enough energy or power to keep the vibrator moving when managing skips and leaps in the melody.

Lip buzzing or tongue trills are a good way to test your air pressure. While buzzing those lips, take note of the feeling in your abdomen. Do you feel resistance maybe similar to when you are lifting something heavy? If so, your expiratory muscles are engaged and are helping to provide consistent air pressure. Work to feel the same way when singing. Now do the lip buzz just below and just above the note that is troubling you. Take note if one pitch requires more air pressure than another. Now take out the buzzing and replace it with a vowel you find takes less effort, maybe it is *ah* [a] or *oo* [u]. Once that gets nice and smooth, sing on the lyrics again.

For those who work well with imagery, you may think about connecting the dots of a circle. Use one continuous line of airflow to create a clean, smooth shape. Remember that the line is constantly moving forward and away from the singer and that you should not let up until the dots are completely connected.

Another possible culprit for the voice crack is a lack of coordination between the registers. Refer back to the section on registration and the *mixed* voice. Strengthening the high and low registrational areas of your voice are a great first step. Then it is wise to approach the mixed voice with ease. Do not wait until you are at the top of your chest voice to try to switch to your head voice, the transition should be started sooner. Likewise, do not wait until you are at the bottom of your head voice before adding some stronger qualities of the chest voice.

Scooping—it was mentioned earlier that scooping is a stylistic character of CWM; however, it should not be the default mode for the singer. For scooping to have the desired effect, it should be used as such, an effect, and not the only method of transition from note to note. The old adage "everything in moderation" is great advice in this case. Here are some ways to work to help the singer learn alternative methods of transitioning between pitches.

> Take any interval, I have perfect fifth here, and focus on singing each note with a slight separation between tones. Use the consonant to help initiate the sound rather than scooping up into the pitch. As this becomes easier, take the consonant away and sing on just a vowel. Feel free to play around with different vowel and consonant combinations.

Tah tah tah   Tah tah tah   Tah tah tah
Ah ah ah   Ah ah ah   Ah ah ah

> This exercise has the same idea with more notes. We now have two different intervals to navigate. Take your time and increase speed as skill allows. Feel free to explore different vowel and consonant combinations.

Da da da da   da da da   Da da da da   da da da

It is always helpful to isolate the problem section of a piece and sing them in a staccato manner (short and precise). Replacing lyrics with one single syllable may also help the pitches be more accurate as there is not time to sing more than one note.

3

CWM Style Is Not . . .

Now that we have discussed the characteristics of the CWM style, it is important to highlight the characteristics that do not fall under CWM. This should help those who have had training in other vocal styles identify some of the technical methods that should be altered in order to achieve a more blended, stylistically CWM sound.

PRONUNCIATION

CWM style is not like classical or choral music when examining the pronunciation of vowels and consonants. Classical music was built on the idea that the melody is paramount and everything else is in service of the musical line. Therefore, the clarity of the lyrics play second fiddle in importance. Due to the lack of microphones, it was also necessary for classical vocalists to maximize the space in the vocal tract to get the most volume achievable by the voice. The result is a style that has very tall, open vowels and minimized consonant articulation. It is a beautiful and full sound that is less conversational than the contemporary world.

Likewise, choral music has a lofty open tone. The central idea is that the entire group blends well and sounds as one. To achieve this, the focus is less on consonants and more on vowels that are open and clear. This is a beautiful sound when employed as a group, but sounds strange and less intelligible when employed as an individual. Remember the goal for contemporary music is to communicate the meaning of the lyrics and be conversational.

AIR CAPACITY

CWM style does not spend much time focusing on the need for a large capacity of air for the singer. Classical, choral, and Musical Theatre singers spend a decent amount of time learning to expand their air capacity and practice using that air quite conservatively (a breathy onset is forbidden). In classical singing this is partially due to the long phrases that are so prevalent and needed for a blended vocal sound, and the air pressure that is required to produce certain pitches and volume levels. This technique may harken back to the idea that the melodic line is the most important element of the song and should be interrupted as little as possible. CWM, as well as other contemporary styles, make use of more frequent breaths to help emphasize the point of the storyline as well as stay true to a conversational quality of signing. While there is still use for expanding the singers' air capacity in any genre, long phrases are not emphasized or needed.

Furthermore, take caution that tension does not enter the picture when preparing for any type of breath. Arneson and Brown note that "most voice scientists and prominent singing teachers agree that the amount of air you take in is far less consequential than how you manage that air."[1] Overfilling or

---

1. Arneson and Brown, *Musical Theatre Voice Pedagogy*, 45.

letting the neck area fill with tension can be more detrimental to a beautiful sound than having to take an extra breath in a phrase.

REGISTERS

Unlike the CWM style, the falsetto and head voice are not considered equals in the classical and choral worlds. The light quality of the falsetto voice is not desired in almost any situation in these two genres. As you may derive from the name, the term falsetto was believed by many classical pedagogues to be a "false voice."[2] It was an undesirable tone quality and very few, if any, were encouraged to use it. Furthermore, it did not have much use as the sound does not carry well without electronic amplification, and of course, we know that such novelties did not exist until the mid-1920s.[3]

The chest register is also rarely encouraged in classical circles. It was once thought (and may still be by some) that the head register is the most pleasing sound and the only healthy way to use the voice. This is not the belief in the singing of any other genre and the singer would lack style should they apply this method of singing in any contemporary style where the vocal range requires otherwise.

PERFORMANCE

In many other musical genres, the purpose of presenting the music is to entertain people. CWM is not about entertainment, not for people or God. This musical form exists to give praise to God, remind people of God's attributes, and in many cases, help people refocus from the worldly issues of their lives and put the

2. Miller, *Structure of Singing*, 120.
3. Hoch, *So You Want to Sing*, 21.

focus on God. Dr. Walter Brath reminds his students that the music presented during a church service is an opportunity for that group of believers to take part in an act of corporate prayer or "sung prayer" (whether it is a praise and celebration, a time of lament, or subdued reflection).[4] Though the words may be put to song, the people of God are collectively praying to him (similar to the content of the book of Psalms). This is a special act that we get to participate in as one family of God. What a wonderful glimpse of heaven this is!

This phenomenon can create inner conflict for the CWM singer. Though we are made to glorify God, our sinful nature is always knocking at the door. It is not difficult to get caught up in the talent you have been given or the skills you have refined and feel proud of the music that you are creating. We are human. It may be a daily task for each musician (as it is for any other person) to remember that leading worship is all about God, and without his presence your efforts will be completely lost.[5]

So how does the singer approach the platform for worship? The keywords are humility and authenticity. In CWM it is not enough to just act as though you are in prayer. The singer should work inwardly to feel and display emotions genuinely. Spend time with the lyrics. What is the composer's main thought? What is the overall message of this song? What does this song mean for you and your relationship with God? All these questions should be examined before you lead others in this musical prayer.

Remember too that we are commanded by the bible to praise God physically as well; through dance (Ps 149:3), kneeling (Ps 95:6), with our hands (Ps 47:2; 63:4), standing (Exod 33:10), and with instruments and singing (Ps 98:5–6). Feeling comfortable enough to outwardly express your inward

4. Walter Brath, interview by author, Nov 21, 2022.
5. Robinson, "Contemporary Worship Singers," 231.

emotions is beneficial to the congregation for a couple of reasons. This is an indication to the people in front of you that you are engaged in the music; they perceive this through your physical actions. Though the music is presented with excellence and the condition of the heart is right, the outward expression helps the congregation to more fully engage in the message you are presenting.

Furthermore, an outward expression is often a show of the overwhelming desires within someone. Just as a person leaps for joy out of pure reflex when they receive good news, a physical show of emotion while worshiping God shows how intense the commitment is. It can also be a sign to those around you that you love God so much you need to do more than just say it with your mouth. This is an invitation to others to dive deep and find a similar experience with their God. While the condition of the heart is still paramount (if the emotion is not really there, don't fake it) an authentic outwardly expression can be a useful tool in guiding others into the presence of God.

So, how do you present the music in a show of excellence and physicality without appearing as a performer? We are all wired differently, we have grown up with different church experiences, and present our emotions in different manners. One person's outward show of worship may be another person's definition of distraction or even excess. Though it is not possible to appease everyone, it is the condition of the heart that should be stressed. If you are truly in a place of worship inwardly, you can rest assured that God knows the condition of the heart, despite what others may perceive. Though some may be offended, I pray that others are encouraged; and if that is not the case, you can take heart knowing that God is pleased with those who are truly in a state of worship and the main goal has been accomplished.

4

Vocal Health

Just as the runner has to care for the body's overall health to continue a task, so the vocalist (professional or layperson) needs to care for the body. Both are physical activities and these imperfect bodies do deteriorate over time. Healthy habits and activities help in slowing this process.

Leon Neto and David Meyer completed a study on the self-reported vocal health of contemporary Christian singers and worship leaders on the international stage. They found that of the different vocal issues that had been reported, laryngitis (swelling of the larynx and often loss of voice) and vocal fatigue topped the list.[1] While both issues can have several different causes, the frequency of vocal fatigue can certainly be mitigated with good vocal health practices.

POSTURE

Hold out your hand in front of your body. For the first minute or two the task is easy. The longer the hand and arm are extended, the harder the muscle has to work. If you were to attempt to

1. Neto and Meyer, "Joyful Noise."

do this all day long, the pain in these muscles would be great. This is similar to what people are doing to their neck and back muscles when held in a position unintended by the design of our body. Though the ever-popular slouch may feel like a more comfortable position, the strain on the body can be great and the neck tension can easily transfer into the voice.

The posture of the singer is important no matter what the genre. Correct alignment helps the body work most efficiently by putting weight on structures that were designed to hold it and relieving tension for muscles that are meant for periodic use. Neto noticed in his study that, though most of the CWM singers had a hunched-over, shoulders-forward stance, those singers who were also instrumentalists (guitarists and pianists) were the worst offenders (likely a direct result of the use of the instrument).[2] Allowing the shoulders to roll forward and the head to protrude beyond the center of the spine, or allowing the spine to curve slightly and compress the abdomen, compromises the body's ability to breathe freely and the muscle's ability to relax properly. The article "Posture and Voice" specifically talks about one such muscle:

> The stylohyoid muscle that connects the hyoid to the base of the skull, shortens. . . . In so doing, in its resting position, it causes the larynx to rise in the neck, thereby changing the shape of the vocal tract, altering resonance and pitch.[3]

Ideal posture is displayed when the knees are slightly bent over the toes, hips are square above the knees, the rib cage hovers over the hips, shoulders are also in line with the hips and are not full of tension, and the head is centered over the shoulders and in line with the spine. This position allows the bone and tendon structures to stabilize the body, allowing the muscles to

2. Neto, "Contemporary Christian Music," 197.
3. Rubin et al, "Posture and Voice," 273.

rest in between isolated actions. Living with good posture can relieve joint pain from the ankles up through the back and into the neck and can provide many other health benefits.[4]

Of course, perfect posture at all times is not a practical proposal. I enjoy curling up in the chair at the end of a long day as much as the next person. But, when possible, and especially during singing, checking and correcting your posture offers many benefits. Indeed, the guitarist faces particular postural challenges due to the placement of their instrument. However, the benefits of straightening the back and neck muscles while playing (though it may require much retraining) will benefit the singer and the whole body.

VOCAL REST

While it is not possible for most singers to only sing when they are feeling in tip-top condition, there are a few indications that the voice requires rest.[5] Certainly, if you cannot produce the music that is expected for that day due to hoarseness or lack of range, the singer should refrain from performing and allow the voice time to recuperate. When the speaking voice is quite hoarse as well, take this as an indication that the vocal folds are not well. Limiting your speech and singing is important at this time to allow for healing.[6] If the throat is in pain while swallowing or talking, listen to the pain and rest the voice. Pain is an indication that something in the body is not right.

Marking during a rehearsal or personal practice time is also encouraged. Notes that are on either end of your range may not cause issue when used occasionally, but they can be problematic if the voice is especially tired or under strain. Avoiding

---

4. Rubin et al, "Posture and Voice," 273.

5. Miller, *Structure of Singing*, 224.

6. Sataloff et al, "Vocal Rest," 560.

such notes, singing gently and less loudly in the core of your range, and avoiding talking loudly are all ways to preserve the voice. These techniques are especially important when preparing for extra periods of voice use such as holidays or special church occasions.

When the symptoms of pain or hoarseness (due to mucus drainage, overuse, or incorrect technique) subside, then the singer can begin using the vocal mechanism again gently, and ease into the more difficult or lengthy demands. It is imperative at this point to use a gentle vocal warm-up to lightly awaken the muscles and blood flow to the vocal folds. This work is not much different from the athlete who has taken some time off to rest an injured body part and stretches gently before resuming training.[7]

It is important to take note of the cause of pain or hoarseness. If the pain is clearly a result of external circumstances (such as a head cold or even overactive allergies) then returning to good vocal technique after the situation is resolved will suffice. If the hoarseness or vocal fatigue is a result of misuse of the voice, then take the next step and consult a voice professional. The issue is likely to continue if the technique is not addressed.

VOCAL ADVICE

There are two types of professionals you may turn to for vocal advice. The first is the vocal instructor. If you sing relatively frequently and regularly struggle with vocal fatigue or hoarseness, it is time to seek advice from a professional vocal instructor. Your technique likely needs a tune-up and doing so will relieve strain and misuse of your voice. While vocal rest for a few hours or more may relieve the symptoms, the recurrence indicates that a bigger issue is at hand. Seeking the advice of

7. Sataloff et al, "Vocal Rest," 560.

a professional will give your irreplaceable instrument a longer lifespan as well as improve your sound.[8]

If you have suddenly experienced a change in your speaking or singing range that doesn't have a clear external cause (like an illness) and that persists for two weeks or more, it would be wise to seek a physician's expertise.[9] This change may be a result of an injury to the vocal folds; seek the opinion of an otolaryngologist or ENT. This is not a time to panic; this does not mean that you have a permanent or serious issue. It simply means that more investigation would help determine the root cause. If a pathology at the level of the vocal folds is discovered, doctors and vocal therapists will be able to give you an overview of the situation as well as a path to healing. Do not assume your vocal injury is the end of your voice.

PRACTICE (NOT JUST WEDNESDAY AND SUNDAY)

The sound we produce emanates from muscles working to move tissue, causing vibrations that interact with the environment. Any time muscle movement is employed, that area of the body benefits from regular and consistent training of those muscles.[10]

> In learning a sport the muscles must be made to perform the same functions over and over so they will learn what they should do automatically. That is why athletes practice daily. And why singers must also.[11]

> Like all athletes and skilled performers, singers must practice in order to maintain and improve their proficiency level. The major goals of practicing are developing

8. Riggs, *Singing for the Stars*, 137.
9. Robinson, "Vocal Health and Voice Care," 1.
10. Sataloff, *Vocal Health and Pedagogy*, 205.
11. Alderson, *Complete Handbook of Voice Training*, 21.

the necessary physical and mental skills for artistic singing, applying acquired skills of singing performance to
artistic expression, and physically and mentally preparing for varying performance situations.[12]

Regular practice is important for the human body no
matter what the nature of the task. The brain must practice the
times tables before they are cemented in the memory, and the
athlete must practice the physical steps before they are expected
to be used in a game; so too the singer must practice vocal techniques, the lyrics, and melody if the voice is to be expected to
be in good shape after thirty minutes or more of vigorous use.
Furthermore, the body needs to be conditioned for the task.
Of course, adding practice to our daily lives is not an easy task
to manage. We all have busy schedules with family and work
and possibly other serving commitments. Do not stress about
it. Add time in when it seems to fit.

If the set of music for an average service is around twenty
to thirty minutes, the voice needs to be trained to meet that
goal. However, you do not have to start there. While singing for
a minimum of thirty minutes at a time would be great, starting
smaller may be better for you. Pick one song and one warm-up
exercise. Focus on those two for ten minutes, refining the notes
and the particular technique you have chosen to work on. Then
reward yourself by just enjoying singing through the piece.
Use the song to praise God. Repeat this several times a week.
Reserve just these ten minutes in your calendar throughout the
week. You may be surprised what that practice time evolves
into.

It is also important to keep the voice in shape even on the
weeks when you are not preparing to lead worship. Feel free to
vary your repertoire. If you do not have to lead worship that
week, venture out and work on songs that you enjoy. Keep them

12. Nix, "Best Practices," 215.

in the same genre or try something new. Variety helps keep things fresh.

Practice in the position in which you plan to perform. Muscle memory (or procedural memory) is an important factor in singing. It is what helps us repeat an action that has been practiced, without having to consciously think about it.[13] Just like riding a bike has become an automatic action for the young child, so too are the activities you perform in the rehearsal space. Remember to practice the communicative factors of the song as well. A singing actor will practice the emotions of the character so that they are more accessible during performance. Likewise, a worship singer (once the basics are learned) will need to connect the emotions with the lyrics to understand the message of the song before the moment of worship leading.[14] Not only does this prepare the brain to be in a worship mindset during the service, but it also prepares the voice for the emotions that may cause physical changes during singing. Dr. Kathy Kessler-Price advises her singers, "Sunday mornings are difficult if you only sing on Wednesday nights and Sunday! If you practice each day, and warm up on your way to services, your singing will be much more effective and enjoyable."[15]

Once we know how often to practice, it is helpful to know what to practice. Singing is always more fun when we are focusing on the areas we do well in, but that is not how a person improves. Practice is most useful when we spend a significant amount of time on areas that are difficult. Isolate those sections, slow them down, and repeat them several times once they are corrected. This helps the brain to remember the correct method, rather than the previous habit. Without this focus, the

13. "Procedural Memory," para. 1.

14. This does not necessarily mean you are planning to "perform" these movements during the service, but it does make you more comfortable should the opportunity arise.

15. Kessler-Price, "Working with Aging Singers," slide 16.

difficult will never progress to mastered. It is also good practice to revisit a section you have corrected after a bit of time has passed. When you put something away, for even ten seconds, the brain has time to process and store the information. You are giving the information time to sink in.[16]

> When struggling with a melodic line, you may find it helpful to remove the lyrics temporarily. Sing your part on a neutral syllable such as *da* [da] or *tee* [ti]. This allows for more attention to the pitches, breath control, and phrasing. Once the struggle eases, add the lyrics back in. Likewise, if lyrics are causing strife, take out the notes. Spend time with just the lyrics. Look for the story or message being told. Often this allows the singer to see the message in a new light and make a personal connection that helps the memory.

Take time to enjoy the areas you do well, get excited about singing, spend some time improving the trouble spots, and end on a high note by reviewing a former accomplishment. Perhaps the most important element of practice is remembering to stay positive. Give yourself grace when something does not go as planned or anticipated. Consider it another slice of information on what to avoid, but do not dwell on it. The more you focus on the bad, the more difficult it will be to form new habits. Stay encouraged by remembering that with each new practice session, you are taking your next steps in your vocal journey.

WARM-UP/COOLDOWN

Let's talk about vocal warm-ups *and* cooldowns. The vocal warm-up is used to "wake up" the voice. Ingo Titze explains it like this: "Rarely does a voice respond instantly after pro-longed silence, sleep, or days of rest. Not only does the instrument

16. Fields, "How Does 'Muscles Memory' Work?," para. 2.

need to be primed, but the player needs to be recalibrated to the instrument."[17]

A good warm-up takes time, time that we often feel we don't have in our everyday lives. However, squeezing in a warm-up during other activities is rarely productive and can be potentially harmful. Dr. Daniel K. Robinson explains that it is never a good idea to consider warming up in the car a sufficient preparation for performance. Though jamming in the car is always fun, and certainly convenient, it does not serve your voice well. Your body is not in a well-aligned position and the acoustics (not to mention the other noises) do not give you an accurate perception of your volume or vocal quality. Robinson states,

> In order for you to hear yourself over the audible levels of the car you need to sing 20dB louder. My van, while idling and with the radio turned off, registers 57dB which means I need to be singing at least 77dB to hear myself. Sustaining this level is counter to the ideals of a good warm-up which necessitates a slow, even, and gradual stretching of the muscles. Singing above 75dB won't assist those ideals.[18]

Robinson also notes that the sound check for the band is not the time for a vocal warm-up. Not only is it not a good use of the band's time, but the sound engineer's job is inhibited as well. The goal of the sound engineer is to set up the levels based on what is needed for your voice when it is at a performance level. If your singing voice is not the same during a sound check as during a performance, the sound check cannot be accurate and the overall sound of the group will suffer. Warming up your voice in a room with minimal ambient noise is a good idea. Find a place where you can hear yourself rather easily and you have some space to move around when needed.

17. Titze, "Warm-Up Exercises," 21.
18. Robinson, "Vocal Warm-Ups," 2.

Though the recommended duration of a warm-up varies from one voice expert to another, the minimum suggestion is ten minutes. Exercises should cover a wide range of pitches for varying lengths of time. The idea is to gently introduce each type of phonation, vowel, and color you intend to use during the impending practice session or performance. One way to remember the guidelines is the acronym *EVENED*: sing every vowel, every note, every day. Though you may not have time for a forty-five-minute practice session every day. Getting in ten minutes of vocalizing in the form of a warm-up is a great start, and who knows, you may be having so much fun a practice session ensues. If you need some suggestions on vocalizes to use during your warm-up, any of the aforementioned exercises will work and can be modified to fit your needs.

In addition to warming up the vocal mechanism, you should warm up the breathing system. The article "How do I Maintain Longevity of My Voice" informs the singer that "exercises that focus on proper breathing and control of respiration during phonation should be employed to help tone the abdominal muscles and prepare them for use in support of phonation."[19] As mentioned previously, the breath is the power source for the voice, giving it a proper warm-up will allow the body to produce sound more efficiently.

To get an idea of how the abdominal muscles assist in breathing for vocal work, stand with correct posture and gently place one hand on the abdomen. Take a deep breath in, (through the nose if possible) allowing the tummy to expand (as it may after a large holiday meal). Once the tummy seems full, release the air in short bursts on an *s* [s] sound. Be conscious of the action your abdominal muscles are, or are not, taking. Proper engagement of these muscles will display a slight contracting,

19. Heman-Ackah et al., "How Do I Maintain Longevity," 468.

or firming,of the abdominal muscles. This is an indication that they are assisting in controlling the air as it is let out. Too much contraction and all of the air escapes (like the unexpected ball to the tummy). No contraction is an indication that the air is escaping with little conscious control. A slight contraction shows that the muscles most equipped with regulating the air output are engaged.

Now that you know what it feels like when those muscles are helping with singing, here is an exercise to use in your warm-ups to prep them for vocal activity.

Take in the same, full breath as before. On the same *s* sound, release it in short bursts of four quarter notes and one whole note. Repeat this four to six times.

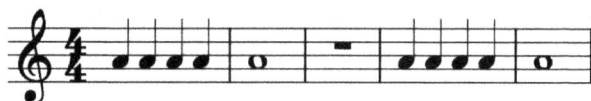

The vocal cooldown is just as important as the warm-up, despite being overlooked often. It helps the body to understand that the rigorous conditioning activity is completed, and it is time to return to a less strenuous and semi-resting posture—particularly for WCM music where the singer's larynx has likely spent significant time in a raised position. Remember that when you create the talky quality voice that has a color of the belt, the larynx is raised. When the singing activity has ceased the voice does well to get a reminder of what the lower resting position should feel like. It consists of vocal activity that is similar in structure to a warm-up, but with less intensity: "The focus here is not to increase tone, but rather to help the vocal muscles achieve a state of healthy relaxation after a day of prolonged use."[20] Some examples of vocal cooldowns are a gentle sighing in a head voice register. You can hum a five-note scale or you can use the low vocal fry for a few seconds. Kari Ragan performed a study in which "the majority of the singers stated that vocal fry resulted in a more relaxed speaking voice."[21]

Ultimately, your warm-ups and cooldowns should be specific to you: "Depending on a singer's individual needs, consideration should be given to the vocal range of each exercise, order of the protocol, and overall length of time spent."[22] Just as each voice is unique, each will come with differing needs. Selecting a few exercises at a time that focus on areas of need for the individual voice will be the most effective. Over time, varying the exercises based on the changing needs of the voice will aid in the growth and the expansion of technique.

HEARING PROTECTION

Protecting your hearing is also a means of protecting your voice. When a singer is flooded with sound or struggles to hear their own voice, they tend to sing louder in an effort to hear themselves more clearly. The louder the surrounding noise, the louder the singer tends to sing, which can result in *pushing* or extra effort in the muscles of the larynx. Singing in a loud environment on a regular basis puts the singer at risk for damage to the vocal folds in and the hearing mechanisms which are quite sensitive. Hearing damage can begin at decibels as low as ninety dBA depending on the length of exposure time. If you suspect that you are being exposed to damaging sound levels, seek out hearing protection. Hearing protection specifically is becoming

20. Heman-Ackah et al., "How Do I Maintain Longevity," 467–72.
21. Ragan, "Efficacy of Vocal Cool-Down," 524.
22. Ragan, "Efficacy of Vocal Cool-Down," 524.

more widely available and can be obtained by contacting an audiologist.[23]

For your reference, take note of the common sounds in your day and their decibel rating. Then notice the duration of exposure OSHA (Occupational Safety and Health Organization) recognizes before damage to the hearing mechanism begins.

dBA	Sound Source
40–43	Refrigerator, Large Office
64–74	Sewing Machine, Power Lawn Mower
75	Electric Shaver
90	Average Motorcycle
95–100	Leaf Blower
100–120	Maximum Output of Stereo
110	Chain Saw
120	Average Snowmobile
140	Average Rock Concert

Table 1[24]

Duration per Day, Hours	Sound Level dBA Slow Response
8	90
6	92
4	95
3	97
2	100
1.5	102
1	105
.5	110
.25 <	115

Table 2[25]

23. McCoy, *Your Voice: An Inside View*, 274–75.
24. Chepesuik, "Decibel Hell," 37.
25. "Safety and Health Regulations," para. 4.

HYDRATION

Keeping the body well hydrated is a recommendation for an overall healthy life, and it undoubtedly applies to vocal health. To vibrate freely and therefore healthily, the vocal folds absolutely require lubrication through hydration.[26] The vocal folds are coated in mucus that helps to lubricate them as they come into contact. Just like the oil in an engine keeps the moving parts from grinding together and damaging each other, this mucus helps to protect the vocal folds from rubbing too powerfully against each other. The less hydrated the body is, the thicker the mucus becomes (throughout the entire body), the less freely it moves, the less protection you receives from the mucus.[27]

How do you stay hydrated? By taking in fluids! Of course, water is a great selection, but fluid intake does not need to be limited to just water. Coffee, tea, and other flavored beverages are all water-based. In addition, fruits and vegetables contribute to the hydration levels of the body. Though it is said that you must consume eight glasses of eight ounces of water per day, this idiom does not take into effect the fluctuations in each person's biology. It is also mentioned frequently that light-colored urine is an indication that you are well hydrated. Though this may be a good guideline, you should consider that the color will fluctuate depending on the volume as well as factors such as medications, vitamins, and other health issues.[28]

Caffeine is a contentious topic. It is prevalent in the literature pertaining to the voice that limiting caffeine, or excluding it completely, is to the benefit of every singer, due to its diuretic effects. Yet, this thought line fails to take into account the fact that these beverages are often water-based, and the volume of

---

26. Heman-Ackah et al., "How Do I Maintain Longevity," 468.
27. Hoch, *So You Want to Sing*, 54.
28. Valtin, "Drink at Least Eight Glasses," R1000-R1001.

THE "VOICE" OF WORSHIP

caffeine that must be consumed to reach a true dehydration effect is at least five cups of coffee per day. Therefore, to exclude these beverages from the count of consumed liquid would discount their value. In addition, there is no scientific evidence that small amounts of caffeine have a significant effect, if any, on the overall viscosity of the mucus surrounding the vocal folds.[29]

There are other factors to consider in a beverage besides caffeine. The sugar content, as well as the dairy content, can influence the voice. Carbonation can affect the digestive tract, and therefore the voice. Of course, not all liquids are created equal and the many ways to stay well hydrated vary depending on the individual. I recommend having a conversation with your physician to determine how best to stay hydrated.

ACID REFLUX

Acid reflux has been known to have detrimental effects on the voice. Acid reflux is a condition that most people want to avoid, but it presents particular difficulty for singers beyond the general discomfort.

> Reflux is the regurgitation of stomach contents into the esophagus and occasionally larynx, throat, and/or nose, and usually occurs when the pressure in the stomach surpasses that of the lower esophageal sphincter, the sling of muscles that are designed to help keep stomach content.[30]

Reflux and heartburn are not one and the same. "Heartburn is a symptom of severe and frequent refluxed gastric acid

29. I would like to note that the detrimental effects of caffeine on the voice are still debated. As one article notes, studies cannot pinpoint their direct effects on the vocal membrane rather than the overall effect on the body; Vishar Bhavsar, "Essay on the Evidence Base." More research should be done in this area.

30. Heman-Ackah et al., "How Do I Maintain Longevity," 470.

into the esophagus."[31] Reflux can occur without heartburn. The problem for vocalists is when the acid that is coming out of the digestive system encounters the larynx. Because the larynx is essentially thinner than the esophagus, the acid can cause damage to the larynx a bit easier than the esophagus. The results can be the following:

> Contact irritation or laryngitis. Such irritation can trigger a cough, a sensation of tickle in the throat, a need for throat clearing, swelling of the vocal folds, a sensation of postnasal drainage or phlegm in the throat; and they can alter sensation (ability to feel) in the larynx.[32]

Acid reflux can be mitigated by altering behavior. Avoiding eating within three hours of lying down for bed can help the stomach acids have adequate time to calm down before the body goes horizontal. Also, you can avoid drinking high volumes of liquid before a performance. Given the higher pressure that occurs in the abdomen during singing (with the movement of the breathing muscles), a full stomach can cause the stomach to leak some acid.[33] The ultimate goal is to keep acid reflux at bay at all times as it affects the esophagus and larynx whether singing or not. Of course, if you suspect this is an issue for you, seek a physician's advice.

31. Heman-Ackah et al., "How Do I Maintain Longevity," 470.
32. Heman-Ackah et al, "How Do I Maintain Longevity," 470.
33. Neto and Meyer, "Joyful Noise," 17.

61

Conclusion

THOSE LEADING WORSHIP SHOULD not be expected to be perfect. Notes will be missed, refrains may be skipped and the voice may crack from time to time. Let's not forget the unexpected and frustrating times when you wake up with hardly any voice at all. Giving yourself and your teammates grace when things do not go right should be expected within the body of Christ.

But we do know that good leaders plan. As a member of your team, you are responsible for your part in preparation for the service (whether you are the sole leader or the supportive vocalist). Your job as the worship singer is not that different from the pastor's job. The pastor helps to guide others in the study of God's word. The worship team is there to facilitate the worship through the songs of the congregants. A singer who is prepared musically, physically, technically, and spiritually will help to remove barriers for both themselves and for those following by ushering people more fully into the presence of God, putting aside outside worries or troubles, and leaning into his character.

God has brought you to this place for a purpose. As the worship leading vocalist, you have been given the heart to help others encounter the Father and the skills to do it through song. These are God-given abilities; go steward them well.

Biography

KELLY MCDOWELL IS AN experienced vocal instructor. With a focus on the intricate world of vocal pedagogy, she has helped many students, young and mature, take their next step in healthy and efficient vocal technique. When not working she enjoys engaging in the lives of her family and friends. Learn more about her work at KFMVoiceStudio.com.

Bibliography

Alderson, Richard. *The Complete Handbook of Voice Training*. West Nyack, NY: Parker, 1979.

Anderson, Catherine, et al. *Essentials of Linguistics*. Hamilton, ON: eCampusOntario, 2018. https://ecampusontario.pressbooks.pub/essentialsoflinguistics2/.

Arneson, Christopher, and Kirsten S. Brown. *Musical Theatre Voice Pedagogy: The Art and Science*. Gahanna, OH: Inside View, 2023.

Bartlett, Irene, and Marisa Lee Naismith. "An Investigation of Contemporary Commercial Music (CCM) Voice Pedagogy: A Class of its Own?" *Journal of Singing* 76.3 (January/February 2020) 273–82.

Benson, Elizabeth Ann, and Elizabeth L. Blades. *Training Contemporary Commercial Singers*. Oxford: Compton, 2020. https://search.ebscohost.com/login.aspx?direct=true&db=cat03997a&AN=RUL.b2187254&site=eds-live&scope=site.

Bhavsar, Vishar. "An Essay on the Evidence Base of Vocal Hygiene." *Journal of Singing* 65.3 (January/February 2009) 285–96.

Blum, Haley. "Music to Their Ears." *ASHA Leader* 21.5 (May 2015). https://leader.pubs.asha.org/doi/10.1044/leader.FTR2.21052016.50.

Borch, Daniel Zangger. *Ultimate Vocal Voyage: The Definitive Method for Unleashing the Rock, Pop, or Soul Singer Within You*. Bromma, Sweden: Notfabriken Music AB, 2005.

Borch, D. Zangger, and Johan Sundberg. "Some Phonatory and Resonatory Characteristics of the Rock, Pop, Soul, and Swedish Dance Band Styles of Singing." *Journal of Voice* 25.5 (September 2011) 532–37. https://pubmed.ncbi.nlm.nih.gov/20926250/.

Chepesuik, Ron. "Decibel Hell." *Environmental Health Perspectives* 113.1 (January 2005) 46–49.

Colby, Meredith. *Money Notes: How to Sing High, Loud, Healthy and Forever*. Minneapolis: Wise Ink Creative, 2017. https://www.scribd.com/read/506892767/.

"Common Noise Levels (dBa)." International Noise Awareness Day. https://noiseawareness.org/infocenter/common-noise-levels/.

Doris Rikkers, et al., eds. *The Wayfinding Bible*. Carol Stream, IL: Tyndale House, 2013.

Elevation Worship. "Graves into Gardens Ft. Brandon Lake | Live | Elevation Worship." YouTube, Mar 13, 2020. https://www.youtube.com/watch?v=KwX1f2gYKZ4.

Fields, R. Douglas. "How Does 'Muscle Memory' Work?" *Psychology Today*, Jun 24, 2021. https://www.psychologytoday.com/us/blog/the-new-brain/202106/how-does-muscle-memory-work.

Gayle, Charity. "Charity Gayle—Thank You Jesus for the Blood." YouTube, Mar 5, 2021. https://www.youtube.com/watch?v=dhU-Omwg2rU.

Heman-Ackah, Yolanda D., et al. "How Do I Maintain Longevity of My Voice?" *Journal of Singing* 64.4 (March 2008) 467–72. https://www.nats.org/_Library/Kennedy_JOS_Files_2013/JOS-064-4-2008-467.pdf.

Hillsong Worship. "King of Kings (Live)—Hillsong Worship." YouTube, Aug 4, 2019. https://www.youtube.com/watch?v=dQl4izxPeNU.

———. "Who You Say I Am—Hillsong Worship." YouTube, Mar 2, 2018. https://www.youtube.com/watch?v=lKw6uqtGFfo.

Hilton, Line, and Alexa Terry. "The Truth about Singing and Hydration." BAST Training, Jun 21, 2021. https://www.basttraining.com/the-truth-about-singing-and-hydration/.

Hoch, Matthew. *So You Want to Sing CCM (Contemporary Commercial Music)*. London: Rowman & Littlefield, 2018.

Jahn, Anthony F. *The Singer's Guide to Complete Vocal Health*. New York: Oxford University Press, 2013.

Kayes, Gillyanne. *Singing and the Actor*. 2nd ed. London: Bloomsbury, 2004.

Kessler-Price, Kathy. "Working with Aging Singers: How to Preserve, Protect, and Improve Mature Singing Voices." Recorded lecture. Westminster Choir College, Lawrence, NJ, 2020.

Lovetri, Jeannette L. "Contemporary Commercial Music: More than One Way to Use the Vocal Tract." *Journal of Singing* 58.3 (February 2002) 249–52.

McCoy, Scott. *Your Voice: An Inside View*. 3rd ed. Gahanna, OH: Inside View. 2019

Miller, Richard. *On the Art of Singing*. New York: Oxford University Press, 1996.

———. *The Structure of Singing: System and Art in Vocal Technique*. Belmont, CA: Wadsworth Group, 1996

Neto, Leon. "Contemporary Christian Music and the 'Praise and Worship' Style." *Journal of Singing* 67.2 (November 2010) 195–200. https://purdue.primo.exlibrisgroup.com/discovery/fulldisplay?context=L&vid=01PURDUE_PUWL:PURDUE&search_scope=MyInst_and_CI&tab=Everything&docid=alma99169197175201081.

Neto, Leon, and David Meyer. "A Joyful Noise: The Vocal Health of Worship Leaders and Contemporary Christian Singers." *Journal of Voice* 31.2 (August 2016) 250. https://www.researchgate.net/publication/306128589_A_Joyful_Noise_The_Vocal_Health_of_Worship_Leaders_and_Contemporary_Christian_Singers.

Ninni Elliot, et al. "What Happens during Vocal Warmup?" *Journal of Voice* 9.1 (January 1994) 37–44.

Nix, John. "Best Practices: Using Exercise Physiology and Motor Learning Principles in the Teaching Studio and the Practice Room." *Journal of Singing,* 74.2 (November/December 2017) 215–20.

Nix, John, et al. "Application of Vocal Fry to the Training of Singers." *Journal of Singing* 62.1 (September 2005) 53–59.

OfficialNATS. "Contemporary Vocal Styles: Demystifying the Pedagogical Process for Pop/Rock—NATS Chat Jan. 2022." YouTube, Jan 18, 2022. https://youtube.com/watch?v=4C_SM3cP50E&si=Zoclcobzaf84_I9P.

Papa, Matt, and Matt Boswell. "His Mercy Is More." YouTube, Aug 15, 2019. https://www.youtube.com/watch?v=JoeAKG3LVCU.

"Procedural Memory." APA Dictionary of Psychology. Last modified Apr 19, 2018. https://dictionary.apa.org/procedural-memory.

Ragan, Kari. "The Efficacy of Vocal Cool-Down Exercises." *Journal of Singing* 74.5 (May/June 2018) 521–26.

———. "The Impact of Vocal Cool-Down Exercises: A Subjective Study of Singers' and Listeners' Perceptions." *Journal of Voice: Official Journal of the Voice Foundation* 30.6 (November 2016): 764.e1–764.e9. https://pubmed. ncbi.nlm.nih.gov/26778328/.

Ramoo, Dinesh. *Psychology of Language.* Victoria, BC: BCcampus, 2021. https://opentextbc.ca/psyclanguage/chapter/the-articulatory-system/.

Redman, Matt. "Matt Redman—10,000 Reasons (Bless the Lord)." YouTube, Jul 5, 2012. https://www.youtube.com/watch?v=XtwIT8JjddM.

Riggs, Seth. *Singing for the Stars: A Complete Program for Training Your Voice.* New York: Alfred, 1980.

Robinson, Daniel Keith. "Contemporary Worship Singers: Construct, Culture, Environment and Voice." PhD diss., Griffith University, 2011. https:// www.djarts.com.au/product/contemporary-worship-singers/.

———. "Improve Your Church Singing and Give God Your Best Vocals." YouTube, Jun 4, 2019. https://www.youtube.com/watch?v=2sgPUTJ5UfE.

———. "Look before You Leap!" *Journal of Singing* 69.2 (November 2012) 193–98. https://search-ebscohost-com.rider.idm.oclc.org/login.aspx?dire ct=true&db=edo&AN=82828037&site=eds-live&scope=site.

———. "Vocal Health and Voice Care." Dr Dan's Voice Studio, 2013. https:// www.djarts.com.au/articles/vocal-health-voice-care/.

———. "Vocal Warm-Ups." Dr Dan's Voice Studio, 2010. https://www.djarts. com.au/articles/vocal-warm-ups/.

Rubin, John S., et al. "Posture and Voice." *Journal of Singing* 60.3 (January 2004) 271–75. https://www.nats.org/cgi/page.cgi/_article.html/Journal_of_ Singing/Posture_and_Voice_2004 Jan Feb.

"Safety and Health Regulations for Construction." Occupational Safety and Health Administration. https://www.osha.gov/laws-regs/regulations/ standardnumber/1926/1926.52.

Saldías, Marcelo, et al. "The Vocal Tract in Loud Twang-Like Singing while Producing High and Low Pitches." *Journal of Voice: Official Journal of the Voice Foundation* 35.5 (September 2021) 1–23. https://www.academia. edu/42880468/The_Vocal_Tract_in_Loud_Twang_Like_Singing_While_ Producing_High_and_Low_Pitches.

Sataloff, Robert Thayer. *Vocal Health and Pedagogy: Science and Assessment.* Vol. 2. 2nd ed. San Diego, California: Plural, 2006. https://archive.org/ details/vocalhealthpedagoooounse/page/n9/mode/2up.

Sataloff, Robert T., et al. "Care of the Professional Voice: Vocal Rest." *Journal of Singing* 75.5 (May/June 2019) 557–64. https://go.gale.com/ps/i.do?id=GA LE%7CA584330502&sid=googleScholar&v=2.1&it=r&linkaccess=abs&i ssn=10867732&p=AONE&sw=w&userGroupName=anon%7Eac462773 &aty=open-web-entry.

Saunders-Barton, Mary, and Norman Spivey. *Cross Training in the Voice Studio: A Balancing Act.* San Diego, CA: Plural 2018.

"Sphincter Muscle." *Encyclopaedia Britannica*, Aug 18, 2017. https://www. britannica.com/science/sphincter-muscle.

Spivey N. "Music Theater Singing . . . Let's Talk. Part 2: Examining the Debate on Belting." *Journal of Singing* 64.5 (May 2008) 607–14. https://www. normanspivey.com/publications/music-theater-singing-lets-talk-part-2. pdf.

Titze, Ingo R. "Belting and a High Larynx Position." *Journal of Singing* 63.5 (May 2007) 57–58. https://go.gale.com/ps/i.do?id=GALE%7CA1631542 60&sid=googleScholar&v=2.1&it=r&linkaccess=abs&issn=10867732&p =HRCA&sw=w&userGroupName=anon%7E6a467b93&aty=open-web-entry.

———."Warm-Up Exercises." *Journal of Singing* 49.5 (May/June 1993) 21. https://www.nats.org/cgi/page.cgi/_article.html/Journal_of_Singing/ Warm_Up_Exercises_1993_May_Jun.

Townend, Stuart. "How Deep the Fathers Love for Us—Stuart Townend." YouTube, May 6, 2012. https://www.youtube.com/watch?v=tzQj7XvKFmA.

TRIBL. "I Thank God (Feat. Maverick City Music and UPPERROOM) | TRIBL." YouTube, Jan 22, 2021. https://www.youtube.com/ watch?v=LM1qrxoHuds.

Valtin, Heinz. "'Drink at Least Eight Glasses of Water a Day.' Really? Is There Scientific Evidence for '8 x 8'?" *American Physiological Society* 283 (November 2002) R993–R1004. https://journals.physiology.org/doi/ pdf/10.1152/ajpregu.00365.2002.

Wickham, Phil. "House of the Lord (Official Music Video)." Apr 9, 2021. https:// www.youtube.com/watch?v=h8uKldEUrPE.

Index

www.ingramcontent.com/pod-product-compliance
Lightning Source LLC
Chambersburg PA
CBHW070023110426
42741CB00034B/2422